The Friday Night Effect

Bloomsbury Methuen Drama
An imprint of Bloomsbury Publishing Plc

An imprint of Bloomsbury Publishing Plc

Imprint previously known as Methuen Drama

50 Bedford Square   1385 Broadway
London   New York
WC1B 3DP   NY 10018
UK   USA

www.bloomsbury.com

**BLOOMSBURY, METHUEN DRAMA and the Diana logo
are trademarks of Bloomsbury Publishing Plc**

First published 2017

© Eva O'Connor and Hildegard Ryan, 2017

Eva O'Connor and Hildegard Ryan have asserted their right under the
Copyright, Designs and Patents Act, 1988, to be identified as authors of this work.

British Library Cataloguing-in-Publication Data
A catalogue record for this book is available from the British Library.

ISBN: PB: 978-1-3500-5886-6
ePDF: 978-1-3500-5887-3
ePub: 978-1-3500-5888-0

Library of Congress Cataloging-in-Publication Data
A catalog record for this book is available from the Library of Congress

Series: Modern Plays

Cover image © Hildegard Ryan

Typeset by Mark Heslington Ltd, Scarborough, North Yorkshire
Printed and bound in Great Britain

To find out more about our authors and books visit *www.bloomsbury.com*.
Here you will find extracts, author interviews, details of forthcoming
events and the option to sign up for our *newsletters*.

Sunday's Child is a London-based Irish theatre company, founded in 2010, run by Eva O'Connor and Hildegard Ryan. The company has toured its work across Ireland, the UK and Australia. Plays produced by Sunday's Child include *Kiss Me and You Will See How Important I Am*, winner of the NSDF Best Emerging Artist Award 2012, *My Name Is Saoirse*, winner of the First Fortnight Award at the Dublin Fringe 2014, an Argus Angel Award at the Brighton Fringe 2015 and the Best Theatre Award at the Adelaide Fringe 2017, and *Overshadowed*, winner of the Fishamble Award for Best New Writing, recently adapted for television with Rollem productions for BBC Three. The TV adaptation of *Overshadowed* was co-written by Eva O'Connor and Hildegard Ryan, and directed by Hildegard Ryan.

Eva O'Connor is a writer and performer from Ogonnelle, Co. Clare. Her plays include *Clinical Lies*, *My Best Friend Drowned in a Swimming Pool*, *Kiss Me* and *You Will See How Important I Am*, *My Name Is Saoirse*, *Overshadowed*, and most recently *Maz and Bricks* (produced by Fishamble and directed by Jim Culleton). Eva has written and performed for theatre, radio and television. She has a degree in English Literature and German from the University of Edinburgh, and an MA in Theatre Ensemble from Rose Bruford College of Theatre and Performance.

Hildegard Ryan is a writer, director and photographer from Skerries, Co. Dublin. She has directed for stage, screen and radio. She has a first-class degree in English Literature and History from Trinity College Dublin, and a Filmmaking Diploma from Central Film School, London. Hildegard does the design work for all Sunday's Child projects.

The Friday Night Effect will premiere at Assembly, George Square, Studios 4 at the Edinburgh Fringe 2017, before touring to Smock Alley as part of the Dublin Fringe 2017.

The Friday Night Effect

To our friends. For always inspiring us, drinking wine with us, and being on our book covers.

Characters

Collette, *vivacious, magnetic, and spontaneous, is the life and soul of the party. She struggles with bipolar disorder, and is renowned for her zest for life, and her off-the-rails manic episodes.*

Jamie *is assertive and straight talking with a dry sense of humour. She works as a PA to an executive of an international gambling company. She prides herself on running a tight ship and always having immaculate shellac nails.*

Sive, *compassionate, confident and intelligent, is a die-hard leftie and the moral compass of the friendship group. She seems strong and enviably 'sorted' but has a troubled past.*

Host, *runs proceedings and collects the votes from the audience.*

Brian, *Collette's boyfriend*
Mike, *Jamie's boss*
Cormac, *one of Sive's clients*
Security Guard
Jerry, *Jamie's soon-to-be stepdad*
Fergal, *Sive's ex*
Man
Guard

Note: All male characters can be played by one actor.

Host   Dear audience. Thanks for coming along. This is Collette. By the end of tonight she'll be dead.

Collette (*on the phone*)   Hi Brian, baby, it's me againnnnn, you haven't answered the phone so I'm just leaving you a message to say: roses are red, violets are blue, you're such a fucking sexy ride I can't believe I date you WOOOO!

Host   Collette has two flatmates. This is Jamie.

Jamie (*on the phone*)   Yes, Mum, I've bought the willy straws. But do you really want L plates? I mean I just feel it's a bit ironic considering you're like sixty – ok fine. I'll grab them after work.

Host   And this is Sive.

Sive (*on the phone*)   Colm, of course I miss you too but you know you really shouldn't be calling me on my personal number. You can book a session on the app as normal ok, you know the rules. Yes I'm looking forward to seeing you too.

The girls freeze.

Host   Tonight you will be faced with a series of choices, choices that decide the fate of our three characters. Tonight we are inviting you to go on a journey with them, to walk a mile, an evening, in their shoes. At key points in the story we will pause proceedings, and ask you to consider their situation, their circumstances, and then answer honestly what you would do in their situation.

We are not asking you what the 'right', morally superior decision might be, but what decision you would make were you in their exact circumstances.

Do we control our own destiny or is choice just an illusion? Let's find out.

Scene One

Jamie (*to audience*)   By one o'clock this afternoon I was the only person left in the office. I shit you not. Two thousand square feet of prime office space. Thirteen execs under one swanky roof and come lunchtime it's a ghost town. That's how I know it's Friday. I can hear my voice echoing in the rafters. Sometimes I order myself around, just to maintain some semblance of routine.

Flashback.

Mike   Jamie, can you book me a later flight on Monday please, I can't miss my daughter's thing. Her (*clicks his fingers repeatedly*) singing recital thing.

Jamie   It's a ballet show I think.

Mike   Is it? Just get me on a later flight will you?

Jamie   If you fly any later you won't make the Jane Morris meeting.

Mike   Christ. I can't miss that, Jamie, you know that. It will jeopardise the whole deal.

Jamie   Ok. In that case you want to stay on the afternoon flight as planned?

Mike   I told you I can't miss her musical, I'll be shot.

Jamie (*to audience*)   I know his credit card details off by heart. I have the keys to the castle. I am the only one who knows him and his wife are spending thousands on IVF and that he listens to Enya on repeat. I know where the bodies are buried. I am expected to 'sort' everything.

Mike   Oh, and can you get me a bigger suite for the Boston trip? There isn't room to swing an iPad in those standard rooms.

Jamie (*to audience*)   Ah, he's taking his mistress with him. Susan O'Reilly, from Fermanagh. He's been banging her for years. Decades. I'm, like, it's grand, Mike. Trust me there's worse things than shagging your secondary school girlfriend. I would know.

Flashback ends.

Sive (*to audience*)   My name is Sive and I am a functioning alcoholic. She says. Laughing. Hahahaha. But genuinely, I can't remember the last night I didn't drink. I think studying does that to you. It makes you outrageously thirsty. Sometimes in the library all I can think of is a large goblet of cold white wine. And within twenty minutes I have to leave. Sometimes I go away, get mildly pissed, go back to the library and snooze at my desk till the next morning. Sometimes I can be surprisingly productive when I'm tipsy. Recently I had to do a six-thousand word essay on the effect of CBT on sufferers of PTSD in comparison to other traditional forms of talk therapy, and I did it in eight hours sipping straight gin from a Costa cup, and I didn't do too shabby. Got a first actually. Anyway if I'm not pissed in the library I'm with clients. And they nearly always bring me booze. Even if it's something a bit gross like whiskey I'll always knock it back. It takes the edge off. It makes time pass. And besides, it's kinda rude not to.

Jamie *and* **Sive** *are at home discussing* **Collette**.

Sive   Have you heard from Colls today?

Jamie   No, but I saw her in the morning. She was acting a bit nuts.

Sive   Oh yeah? I was actually thinking she's in good form lately.

Jamie   I dunno . . . she got up at like 6 a.m. to go the farmers' market. She came back with a shit ton of organic kale and started shoving it into the blender? Going on about how the antioxidants are going to boost her metabolism and balance her hormones and some shit? She had the radio on full blast, and when I came down she was blitzing it to fuck, with no lid on!

Sive   Oh my God! Is that what the green stains all over the walls were? I spent a good twenty minutes scrubbing them off, christ..I guess it's good she's focussing on her health . . . better than living on tangy cheese Doritos like she used to.

Jamie   Ok, I might be being paranoid but I think she's acting a bit, I hate to say it – manic?

Sive   What like . . . episode manic?

Jamie   I dunno, I'm so bad at judging these things.

Sive   Well I know she started on new meds recently, and it will probably take a while for them to settle in. It's always a bit dodgy at the start isn't it?

Jamie   I guess. I think she's missing being at work and having a proper routine and it's making her a bit . . . I dunno . . . hyper? I know it sounds bad but I just can't cope with unstable Collette right now. I'm up to my eyes with Mum's fricking wedding, and when she's manic, I find her so stressful to be around.

Sive   Ughh, you have me worried now. Ok so don't freak out (*In a conspiratorial whisper.*) but I saw her ASOS order yesterday. Her receipt thing was on the floor beside the bin. She spent 400 quid on clothes in one go.

Jamie   What! She's not even working!

Sive   I know, it's madness. But it might just be impulse buying, or maybe Brian foots the bill . . . She was talking about going out tonight, but let's just stay in, have tea and chats and make sure everything is good with her meds and all.

Jamie Yeah . . . good idea, let's just stick on a movie and chill. Keep her away from the booze.

Sive Yas, I haven't had a night in in ages. Just promise me we're not watching *The Lion King*. She is so obsessed! If I hear 'Circle of Life' one more time I swear I will flip my lid. She fucking sings it, massacres it, in her room 24/7.

Jamie In fairness I've heard a lot worse things than *Lion King* coming through those walls. You missed out on some serious drama last night. Brian was over.

Sive Oh yeah?

Jamie The pair of them were having a full-on screaming match. Colls was hysterically crying by the end.

Sive You serious?

Jamie It was so loud I was this close to going to Jerry's. Where were you last night anyway?

Sive Eh, in the library.

Jamie What all night?

Sive Pretty much, assignments you know.

Jamie You're more insane than Collette.

Collette *enters.*

Collette Who's more insane than me? No one's more insane than me. I AM QWWWWWWWWEEEEEN OF INSANE!

Sive Hey, love.

Collette Good news, chicas!

Sive What?

Collette I'm cured!

Sive Of what?

Collette   Of everything. I'm myself again. I am as stable as this table.

Sive   Great . . . since when?

Collette   Since my new medication.

Jamie   The stuff you started two days ago?

Collette   Yip. Praise be to sweet baby jeez. I finally found some chemicals that work for me. I woke up this morning and I felt incredible. You know when it dawns on you that you are this living breathing seeing feeling thing and the world is yours to experience. I woke up this morning and I thought, the world is my lobster! Lend me some neighbour, I am your sugar! You know?!

Jamie   Eh not really, to be honest, but I'll take your word for it.

Collette   Not in a manic way, before you lose your precious marbles. In a cool calm collected Collette way! I'd like to make a *Collette* call to the US of A please. Hello, yanks? Blow your *trump*-ets! I'm cured! Speaking of America, me and Brian are going to New York in three weeks' time!

Jamie   What?!

Collette   I KNOW! I am gonna eat my weight in Reese's peanut butter everything.

Jamie   Wow. Who's paying for that?

Collette   I am. Back to work on Monday, bitches! I went in today for an hour. To assure them all I'm compos mentos and still shit hot at my job.

Jamie *and* **Sive** *exchange a look.*

Jamie (*to audience*)   Collette *is* shit hot at her job. Normally. She was made for advertising. She's able to talk all that wacky creative shit, and they interpret her inability to focus on anything for longer than two minutes as a 'natural talent for multi-tasking'. It's cut throat though . . . last month when she was acting, excuse my French, totally insane, they were

gonna let her go but Sive fought her corner, and they gave
her paid leave. Collette can be really difficult to live with
when she's having a bad episode. That's when I started
staying with Jerry, my mum's fiancé. He has a really nice flat
in town for work, and I was having trouble sleeping because
Colls was keeping me up, so he offered me a room in his
place a few nights a week. And that's when I sort of . . .
started sleeping with him.

Collette   Girls, come on, let's celebrate my imminent return
to the rat race by going to Spar and buying a fuck ton of gin!

Jamie   Ah Collette, I want to take it easy tonight, it's my
Mum's hen do tomorrow.

Collette   Oh my God the hen's tomorrow? Baawk baaawk
baaawk! Are you psyched?

Jamie   We're going on one of those package hens to Carrick
on Shannon – where you have to hunt for chocolate dildos
in pubs that charge fifteen euro in, and a local farmer
stripping on the bar is the in-house entertainment. It's going
to be amazingly cringe.

Sive   It'll be hilarious. You'll get drunk with a crowd of fifty-
year-old women. You'll come home with some scandalous
stories I'm sure.

Collette   Is silver-fox Jerry having a stag?

Jamie   Dunno.

Collette *takes a bottle of champagne out of the fridge.*

Collette   Ooooh bubbly!

Sive   Colls don't please, that's mine.

Collette   This has been in the fridge for about a year.

Sive   I'm saving it. It's worth eighty quid.

Jamie *and* **Collette**   Eighty quid?

Sive   Yeah. I won it, in a raffle in college.

(*To audience.*) I didn't win it. Cormac gave it to me. Cormac is definitely one of my weirder clients – but before you get all riled up don't worry, he's not a fister, a feeder, a foot lover or any of that freaky stuff. Cormac has a taste for an ultra realist version of the FGE – also known by us gals in the trade as the Full Girlfriend Experience. For most clients, the FGE service is pretty straightforward. Dress code: white lingerie, flowery dress, high heels. Clock starts when you turn up at the door, all smiles and straightened hair, then it's simple wine, chats, massage, blow job, intercourse, spooning, rounded off by the three key words 'I love you'. And then what do you know? Time's up.

The thing about Cormac is, he has a very specific taste – we've met four times now and I've nailed just how he likes it.

Flashback.

Sive *is standing at* **Cormac***'s door.*

Sive   The outfit: frumpy office clothes, hair pulled back, tired and cranky expression. Ding dong . . .

Cormac *answers.*

Cormac   Hi baby, how was your day?

Sive   Ugh a bit shit. I'm so wrecked.

Stomping into the house.

Cormac   Don't I get a kiss hello?

Sive   Jeez, calm down. (*To audience.*) Note palpable disinterest.

She kisses him vaguely on the cheek.

Cormac   Hey, I've made some dinner for us if you fancy it, babe. Carbonara. Your favourite.

Sive I'm not really hungry to be honest, I don't feel very well. And I've got a pounding headache. Anyway, we always have pasta. I'm sick of it.

Cormac Hey come here for a second, honey –

Sive Look I'm not in the mood ok? I'm going to lie down.

Cormac *grabs her arm and drags her to him, with masculine authority.*

Cormac When I say come here you do what you're told, you understand?

Sive's *hand travels up and down* **Cormac**'s *chiselled abs. Her eyes widen.*

Sive (*to audience*) Affronted, yet strangely aroused . . . (*To* **Cormac**.) Cormac . . . have you been working out?

Cormac *lifts* **Sive** *onto him.*

Sive But . . . what about *I'm A Celebrity . . Get Me Out of Here!*?

Cormac (*huskily*) I've set the Sky Box to record.

Sive (*her eyes aflame with passion*) Oh, Cormac!

Flashback ends.

Jamie Is it recommended that you drink on your new meds?

Collette J – J I'm finneee I haven't felt this good in months.

Jamie You're insane.

Collette And that's why you love me. You want to kiss me . . . You want to touch me . . .

She kisses **Jamie**.

Jamie Get off me, you slobbery wench.

Collette   Come on, we have to go to the shop before ten!
Tick tock. Tick tock. Guinness is good for you. Drinks are on
me. (*To* **Sive**.) You, my sweet prince, would drink paint
stripper, don't even lie (*To* **Jamie**.) and Jamie trust me, a few
pints tonight will take the edge off seeing your mum
grinding on a semi-naked twenty-one-year-old farmhand
tomorrow in Carrick on Shannon.

Sive   I'm having a night off the paint stripper.

Jamie   Me too. I'm hitting the tea. Hard.

Collette   Girls, come on. I just really want to celebrate. I
feel like I've been living under a rock for the last few weeks
and I want to let my hair down with my gorgeous gals!

Jamie   Over a nice cup of Barry's?

Collette   I'm trying to make a point here. Look. I know
that I'm sometimes not the easiest person to live with . . .

Sive *and* **Jamie** (*to audience*)   LOL.

Collette   But I want you to know I really appreciate you
putting up with my spaz attacks and being the greatest
friends in the world. We don't have to get trashed! We can
just have a few civilised glasses of wine. And celebrate being
alive!

The **Host** *enters and asks the audience to make the following choice.*

Choice 1:

Option A) Drink with Collette

Option B) Refuse

Option A) Drink with Collette

Sive   Fine! Fine! I give in.

Collette   Woohoo party time!

Sive Note to self: grow a backbone.

Collette *is lying on the floor, texting.*

Sive Who you texting Colls?

Collette Brian.

Jamie What? What happened to our girls' night?

Collette We're blowing off steam aren't we? I've texted Brian to bring his friend Charlie along . . . if you know what I'm saying!

To audience.

Sive Brian is Collette's boyfriend.

Jamie If I had to describe him in one word, I'd say he's –

Sive The worst.

Jamie I mean he is quite laddish.

Sive He's a fucking snake in the south Dublin grass

Jamie He's the kind of guy who got a cap playing for Leinster under fourteen, and never shuts up about it.

Sive He's the kinda guy who yells at women from the front seat of his best mate's beamer.

Jamie I know he can be a bit of a dick sometimes. But he's so loyal to Collette, she is pretty high maintenance, and he is always there for her in her hour of need.

Sive He fucking loves it when she's a mess, because the more needy and pathetic she is the more it boosts his ego. That's not loyalty.

Jamie He spoils her! Remember last year for her birthday he took her out for a meal in a Michelin-star restaurant.

Sive Yeah and when she came down the stairs in her new birthday dress he just shot her this look. She was crushed.

Jamie Oh come on, it was so short!

Sive   It was so her!

Jamie   He's just protective. He has her best interests at heart, even if . . .

Sive   He's controlling. She shrinks when she's around him. She goes all meek and girly like a quiet little housewife –

Jamie   Don't we all act differently when we're in love?

Brian *enters, hugs the girls, hugging* **Jamie** *for slightly too long.*

Brian   Alright, ladies, what's the craic? Jamie, love the sexy secretary outfit, but it's not Halloween till October, babes.

Jamie   Oh fuck off, Brian, I'm just in the door from work.

Brian   Ah you're working the streets these days is it? Fair play. I hear there's good money in it.

Sive   Wow.

Collette   Shut up, Bri. Where are the cans I ordered please?

Brian   Right here, baby. So are you girls getting off your tits tonight or what?

Sive   If, by that you mean, are we having a few civilised drinks just us gals. Then the answer is yes.

Brian   Just us gals. Please. Lucky for you, Brian is feeling particularly generous, cos he got a hefty bonus in work today, and spent it all on booze for the ladies!

Collette   Oh my God, Brian! Baby! Well done! I can't believe you got it.

Brian   Course I got it. Demanded it. Threatened to walk if they didn't cough up. Go hard or go home, ain't that right baby?

He kisses **Collette**. **Jamie** *interrupts.*

Jamie   I can't hack this. Put us all out of misery then.

Brian   What?

Jamie   Give me a fucking drink.

Brian   Ah she's thirsty! I knew we could count on you, you party animal. What about you Sive? Wait don't tell me, you've an 'essay' due.

Sive   Yep I'm just a chronic dry shite with zero social skills. I wish I could be more like you, Brian.

Collette (*smoothing things over*)   Sive is well able to balance academia and alcohol trust me. Girl! I insist.

She hands **Sive** *a can.*

Jamie   Right, Colls, what's the master plan for tonight then, you mad bitch? Now that you've led us astray?

Collette   Well I was thinking, now that we're all up for the sesh, why don't we drink at home for a bit, have a bit of a bop to Fleetwood Mac and then –

Brian (*cutting across* **Collette**)   Fleetwood Mac? Spare me. I'll tell you what we're doing tonight. We're hitting up Rubex.

Jamie   Rubex?

Brian   Don't tell me you haven't heard of Rubex. Of course you fucking haven't.

Sive   Isn't that the crusty new place on the quays? It used to be a box factory or some shit and they're trying to pull it off as warehouse chic?

Brian   It's an old fire station actually, and it's off the chain. State of the art sound system, incredible DJs. I can't believe you girls haven't been there yet.

Collette   Oo let's go! I heard it's like the future of the Dublin techno electro scene. Apparently it's like *the* place to be.

Sive   The place to get ripped off. I'm sorry, I'm not paying 12 euro for a warm rum and coke served out of a jam jar.

Brian   Simmer down love. I know the guys running it. They're good guys. It's the launch tonight. They'll sort us out, guestlist, free champers, the works.

Jamie (*in a south Dublin accent, slagging* **Brian**)   Noice!

Collette   It will be epic. We can have a proper dance, and theres a class DJ line up. Jamie, we might find you a date for your Ma's wedding!

Brian   Absolutely Jamie, you'll pull no bother in that outfit trust me.

Jamie *licks her finger indicating smoking,* **Sive** *rolls her eyes.*

Collette   *And* Bri's brought a bit of fairy dust to help us get on the vibe haven't you Bri?

Brian   You better believe it girls. I've got a bag of Dublin's finest Vitamin C and it's going to blow your tiny minds. No charge. My treat.

Sive *and* **Jamie**   No way!

Option B) Refuse

Collette   You're so fucking boring I can't even deal.

Sive   Overruled sorry,

Jamie   I'll make you some tea.

Collette   Fuck your teetotalling tea! When did you both become minus craic? Is this some kind of protective bullshit? I told you, guys, I am feeling fine and I want to let my hair down. I don't need you to babysit me!

Sive   Colls, course not, we're just not feeling it that's all!

Collette   Whatever.

She flounces off to get her phone. **Jamie** *and* **Sive** *exchange glances.*

Sive   Who you texting, Colls?

Collette   Brian.

Jamie   What? What happened to our girls' night?

Collette   Well since you guys won't party with me, I've had to look elsewhere. Brian's on his way over now.

To audience.

Sive   Brian is Collette's boyfriend .

Jamie   If I had to describe him in one word, I'd say he's –

Sive   The worst.

Jamie   I mean he is quite laddish.

Sive   He's a fucking snake in the south Dublin grass.

Jamie   He's the kinda guy who got a cap playing for Leinster under fourteen, and never shuts up about it.

Sive   He's the kinda guy who yells at women from the front seat of his best mate's beamer.

Jamie   I know he can be a bit of a dick sometimes. But he's so loyal to Collette, she is pretty high maintenance, and he is always there for her in her hour of need.

Sive   He fucking loves it when she's a mess, because the more needy and pathetic she is the more it boosts his ego. That's not loyalty.

Jamie   He spoils her! Last year for her birthday he took her out for a meal in a Michelin-star restaurant.

Sive   Yeah and when she came down the stairs in her new birthday dress he just shot her this look. She was crushed.

Jamie   Oh come on, it was so short!

Sive   It was so her!

Jamie   He's just protective. He has her best interests at heart, even if . . .

Sive   He's controlling. She shrinks when she's around him. She goes all meek and girly like a quiet little housewife –

Jamie   Don't we all act differently when we're in love?

Brian *enters, hugs the girls, hugging* **Jamie** *for slightly too long.*

Brian   Alright, ladies, what's the craic? Jamie, love the sexy secretary outfit, but it's not Halloween till October, babes.

Jamie   Oh fuck off, Brian, I'm just in the door from work.

Brian   Ah you're working the streets these days is it? Fair play. I hear there's good money in it.

Sive   Wow.

Collette   I missed you so much! I'm so excited to go out tonight! With you! (*She kisses him passionately.*)

Jamie   I thought we were taking it easy tonight, Colls?

Brian (*ignoring* **Jamie**)   So are you girls getting off your tits or what?

Sive   If by that you mean are we partying tonight, then the answer is no.

Brian   Don't be such a dry shite, Sive. Wait don't tell me, you've an essay due.

Sive   Yip I'm just a chronic dry shite with zero social skills. I wish I could be more like you, Brian.

Brian   I'm afraid I'm not gonna take no for an answer. Brian is feeling particularly generous, cos he got a hefty bonus in work today, and spent it all on gear for the ladies!

Collette   Oh my God, Brian! Baby! Well done! I can't believe you got it.

Brian   Course I got it. Demanded it. Threatened to walk if they didn't cough up. Go hard or go home, ain't that right baby?

Collette   Yes yes yes! We have to celebrate! Tonight is gonna be off the scales.

Jamie (*privately, with* **Sive**)   This is bad. She shouldn't be going out in this state.

Sive   Well it's a bit late for that now. We have to go and keep an eye on her.

Jamie   Ugh. Fine. (*To* **Collette**.) Right, Colls, what's the master plan then, you mad bitch? Now that you led us all astray?

Collette   Well I was thinking, now that we're all up for the sesh, why don't we get glammed up, have a bit of a bop to Fleetwood Mac and then –

Brian (*cutting across* **Collette**)   Fleetwood Mac? Spare me. I'll tell you what we're doing tonight. We're hitting up Rubex.

Jamie   Rubex?

Brian   Don't tell me you haven't heard of Rubex. Of course you fucking haven't.

Sive   Isn't that the crusty new place on the quays? It used to be a box factory or some shit and they're trying to pull it off as warehouse chic?

Brian   It's an old fire station actually, and it's off the chain. State of the art sound system, incredible DJs. I can't believe you girls haven't been there yet.

Collette   Oo let's go! I heard it's like the future of the Dublin techno electro scene. Apparently it's like *the* place to be.

Sive   The place to get ripped off. I'm sorry, I'm not paying 12 euro for a warm rum and coke served out of a jam jar.

Brian   Simmer down, love. I know the guys running it. They're good guys. It's the launch tonight. They'll sort us out, guest list, VIP section, the works.

Jamie (*in a south Dublin accent, slagging* **Brian**)   Noice!

Collette   It will be epic. We can have a proper dance, and there's a class DJ line-up. Jamie, we might find you a date for your ma's wedding!

Brian   Absolutely, Jamie, you'll pull no bother in that outfit trust me.

Jamie *licks her finger indicating smoking.* **Sive** *rolls her eyes.*

Jamie   You're not wrong, Brian.

Sive   I can't believe we're going to Rubex, Jesus.

Jamie   Sive, didn't you hear, it's *the place*.

Collette   Preach, girl. *And* Bri's brought a bit of fairy dust to help us get on the vibe haven't you, Bri?

Brian   You better believe it, girls. I've got a bag of Dublin's finest vitamin C and it's going to blow your tiny minds. No charge. My treat.

Sive *and* **Jamie**   No way!

Scene Two

In the queue for the club.

Jamie (*to audience*)   So it's a couple of lines later and we're in the queue for Rubex. The lad in front of me is wearing trendy ankle grazer trousers up to his nipples and has brought his fucking grey hound out for attention. Enough said.

Sive   I can't believe we have to queue for this dive.

Brian   This *dive* is Dublin's best kept secret. I know the guys running it, real good guys, and they've got huge plans for this place.

Collette   Can we not skip the queue, baby? If you have friends in such high places, can't you just pull a few strings?

Brian   I'll pull your strings if you're not careful.

He and **Collette** *kiss.*

Sive   Romance is not dead.

Jamie (*to audience*)   And as I'm averting my eyes from the passionate couple I spot these two girls outside the club, sitting on the curb in these tiny barely there glitzy dresses, and *runners*. You know the kids these days wouldn't be caught dead in heels. I'm, like, why couldn't we have been born ten years later? Anyway, these two girls are clearly fucked out of their tree already, massive pupils, talking to each other with this ferocious concentration, having these really intense chats. And there's something about them that takes me back to when we were at that stage, in first year of college. It feels like decades ago.

Flashback.

Collette *and* **Jamie** *are fucked outside a club, back in the day.*

Collette   It just makes me sad that everyone is so afraid of people with mental health stuff going on. Like it makes sense, you're scared of what you don't know but if people are brave enough even just to ask, then they realise that at the end of the day we are all just humans dealing with shit, you know?

Jamie (*finally uninhibited in her yippedness*)   Oh my God I know! Like I don't know why it's so awkward?! Like I've always wanted to ask if you're ok, like what's going on with you, cos I know you were off college for like two months and people were saying vague things but everyone is afraid to ask you, you know? And you're such a happy, amazing person but then you have these like bad patches? How long have you, like, I mean did you always have these mental health things?

Collette   Ok, let me tell you the story. It all began when I was eleven years old. That's when I knew I was different.

Jamie (*listening intently*)   Ok . . .

Collette   I was in my room in the dead of night, when . . . Dumbledore appeared to me with a letter.

Pause. Then hysterical laughter.

Jamie   Oh my God shut up!

Collette   Haha ok. So you know I'm bipolar right?

Jamie   Eh, no. I mean. Kind of. Oh God, Colls, I'm sorry I'm so bad at this kind of shit.

Collette   Babes, relax what are you on about. (*Holding* **Jamie***'s face.*) You are amazing.

Jamie   So that's like what, like some kind of depression?

ColletteS   It's a bit more complicated than that. I'm a complex kind of gal.

Jamie   Oh my God you totally are. That's what I love about you.

Collette   Essentially it's like extreme highs and lows. Like as you know sometimes I can go through like really down times, like I have no energy, and it's all too much for me, I can't even read or do anything. Like I'll just stare at the back of a cereal box and I can't even fucking read snap crackle and pop, cos I'm just too out of it. It's like this horrible horrible weight is pressing on your chest and on your whole life and yeah. Getting up is not even an option. Just existing feels so fucking hard.

Jamie   Colls, that's horrific. I, I can't even begin to imagine.

Collette   And that's only the half of it. I'll get through my down time, and like take my meds and get back on the horse, blah blah, and then like months, or sometimes years later, I'll start to feel kinda weird, kinda like I've taken something and I'm coming up. And then I'll have what they call an 'episode'.

Jamie   An episode . . .?

Collette   Like an episode of *House of Cards*.

Jamie   No way . . .

Collette   Haha you are actually such a dope it's hilarious. I mean like an episode of, like, bad mental health.

Jamie *keels over giggling*.

Jamie   Ok ok, I'm listening. So, like, what's an 'epsiode' when it's not on fucking Netflix. (*Slapping* **Collette** *in jest.*)

Collette   Ok, ok, it's basically like this really really intense high. My mind goes into overdrive, and I have like a million thoughts, and ideas, and sometimes I can't even get my words out. You feel sort of overwhelmed and euphoric at the same time. It's like taking six pills at once, when no one else is on anything. It's pretty awkward.

Jamie   It sounds kinda great.

Collette   Ha ya I know it sounds like great craic, but in real life it's generally a fucking mess. I remember when I was seventeen. I was babysitting my twelve-year-old cousin Nick for the weekend. Anyway I decided we should go out for dinner in this fancy new restaurant that had just opened down the road. I put on this silk nightie thing of my mum's, and gelled little Nick's hair. Took him out as my cute little man date. Anyway when I asked for a table the waiting staff were looking at us kinda funny, like who are these eccentric kids, but I just blagged it, said I was a food blogger, and then they were falling over themselves to make sure we had a great time. I ordered loads of expensive seafood shit and a shit tonne of white wine. And proceeded to get smashed. And then the waiting staff started getting weird and aggro, and Nick started crying, and I couldn't hack it so I just left. Without paying, obviously.

And I just remember running along by the canal, in my bare feet, with this bottle of champagne in my hand, in this pink nightie, screaming into the night feeling higher than I've ever felt before or since. You feel like you're in a film, like you're gliding, like you know you're skating on the thinnest ice, but you feel so invincible you sure it will never, ever break. Until until it does.

Jamie   Shit.

Collette   Yeah they found me under a bridge, miles away at like six the next morning. They being the guards.

Jamie   Christ, Colls, that's dark.

Collette   Yeah. And Nick's mam, my aunt, she didn't speak to our family for like two years after. Because she was afraid that I was some kind of monster. People are so scared of it. Like 'mental illness'.

And I know that the reason that mental health shit has such a bad rep is cos people who are going through stuff can be a fucking nightmare, I will put my hands up and admit I can be a massive fucking pain in the vagina sometimes.

Jamie *giggles.*

Collette   But it's really not me you know. It's just something I'm going through. I am not bipolar. I just have bipolar disorder. Am I making sense?

Jamie (*getting emotional*)   Ya OMG totally. You're inspiring you know that. Like I just feel so much love for you right now. You're actually incredible.

Collette   Promise me, no matter what happens you'll never be scared of me?

Jamie   I will never be scared of you

Collette *leans in and kisses* **Jamie**.

Jamie   Ok now I'm a bit scared of you!

Flashback ends.

Brian, **Jamie** *and* **Sive** *enter the club.*

Sive (*to audience*)   After a queue of twenty minutes we're finally inside. And the second we cross the threshold I am certain it was worth the wait. The smell of sweat and alcohol and vomit hits us like a bus. We pay five euro an item to know that our possessions will be half-supervised by an attendant that looks at me like she genuinely wants me to die. Or to die herself. Either would do. We trek across the sticky dance floor to the bathrooms, which overflow out the door making a nice water feature in the hallway, and then we join the ten-row-deep queue for the bar, at which point I get winked at by a gurning seventeen-year-old boy with a look in his eyes that says 'I just got my braces off today and I am gagging for the shift'.

Jamie   So this is the famous Rubex . . .

Brian   Alright, ladies, let's get this party started! Can I grab three Jägerbombs, a pint of Heino and two skinny G&Ts for my ladies.

Sive   Jeez, Brian, where do you get off ordering for us?

Brian   It's called chivalry.

Jamie   And skinny G&Ts? What the fuck are you trying to say?

Brian   Ah, girls, give it a rest, I'm buying so shut up and drink up.

Sive   I genuinely don't know if I can hack this. Why does It smell like a barn in here? Do there really need to be so many lasers?

Collette   I have heard enough of your negativity, granny Sive. You are coming with me to the bathroom. (*To* **Jamie** *and* **Brian**.) Excuse us while we powder our noses.

In the queue for the toilet.

Sive   You have to hand it to Collette. Only she could make the queue for the toilets seem like the greatest rave of the decade.

Sive *and* **Collette** *are bopping to the techno beat.*

Collette   Dance! Dance! Dance! Then you won't pee your pants! When I'm grooving like this! I hardly need to piss! Everybody bop with me! You'll forget you need to wee!

Sive   Girl! You should be an MC, you've got skillz!

Collette   My God how good is this beat. It's incredible. I can feel the bass vibrating all my organs!

Sive   You know what, Colls, it's starting to grow on me.

Collette   We're next! Yas!

They go into the cublicle.

Party timeeee! (*She pulls out the baggie hidden in her bra.*)

I paid double to get really pure shit. It's come all the way from Cuba!

Sive   Cuba?

Collette   Colombia? Canada? Who cares!

Sive   Hey, Colls, it's so great to hang out with you. How are you feeling these days? I know you were having some issues with your new meds and stuff.

Collette   Baby girl, I am great, meds are great, everything is great! I've never felt so alive! Collinator is *back* and we are going to have the night of our lives!

There's a knock on the door.

Security Guard   Open up!

Girls   Oh shit.

Jamie *is at the bar.*

Jamie (*to audience*)   So I'm left at the bar trying to distract Brian as Collette and Sive head off into a cloud of dry ice.

Brian   Some vibe in here!

Jamie   Yeah it's alright actually! I take it all back. Although I was half hoping there's still be some half-naked firemen wandering around.

Brian   Ah they're long gone. I think their pole is still knocking around somewhere though, if you fancy having a little twirl on it.

Jamie   You wish, Brian. So . . . how's work going?

Brian   Ah you know, the usual. Closing deals, making it rain . . . How are things your end?

Jamie   Ah fine, same old same old.

Brian   You still at KRP? What are you on over there?

Jamie   How about none of your business, Brian! I mean obviously the money could be better but it's fine, and it's not for ever. I'm not planning on being a PA all my life.

Brian   Oh no?

Jamie   I'm gonna do my MBA actually. I practically run the show over there anyway. I'm going to move on to bigger and better things.

Brian   Ah fuck the MBA. Effort. You know what you should do? Come be my PA, I'll sort you out with a serious raise!

Jamie   Oh wow, bigshot! Have they made you a partner already?

Brian   Ah not yet, but its only a matter of time. And anyway, I think we'd have a lot of fun working together.

He gropes **Jamie**. *She pushes him off in shock.* **Collette** *and* **Sive** *come back from the bathrooms.*

Sive   Oh my God, guys, me and Collette totally got caught in the cubicles together!

Jamie   Oh shit!

Sive   Collette tried to pretend that we were getting with each other, but they were so on to us. We got frogmarched down to their grim little office to get frisked.

Brian   Ah what? They didn't find the stuff did they?

Collette (*seems subdued*)   No it's here.

Jamie   You ok, Colls?

Collette   Yeah I'm fine, it's just the security guy, when he was frisking me, he kind of put his hand, like, up my skirt, like properly up?

Sive   Hang on what, are you serious?

Collette   Yeah like, it was so weird, he was, like, 'you can't be too careful', I didn't know what to do so I just froze.

Jamie   Oh my God what? That is so not ok, a male bouncer shouldn't even be allowed to frisk women in here. We have to report him!

Brian   A fuck's sake, the Feminazis strike again. Making drama out of absolutely nothing! He was just doing his fucking job. You're alright, babe, aren't ya?

Collette   Yeah I guess I'm fine, it's just . . .

Brian   You're just overreacting. Let's get you a drink and put a smile back on that gorgeous face.

Collette   Yeah I . . . it's probably not a big deal.

Jamie *pulls* **Collette** *aside.*

Jamie   No screw that. I'm sorry but he is paid to make people feel safe not sexually harass women in the club!

Collette   Ah, girls, I don't want to cause a fuss, Brian's probably right maybe he didn't mean to –

Jamie   No Collette! We need to report him! We haven't just paid fifteen Euro in to get creeped on. I'm sick of just putting up with men perving, and getting away with it!

Collette   Maybe I gave him the wrong idea or something? I don't wanna make a big deal out of it.

Sive   In fairness, this kind of stuff happens all the time in clubs. Like it totally sucks but at the same time you have to pick your battles. If we have to go get the manager and he denies it, it'll get really messy. And he obviously knows that we were taking stuff as well. I think we're better off to forget about it and enjoy our night.

Collette   You're probably right.

Jamie   You're seriously gonna let this go?

Sive   Fuck him! He's not even worth the stress.

*The **Host** enters and asks the audience to make the following choice.*

Choice 2:

Option A) report

Option B) don't report

Option A) report

Jamie   Mission accomplished!

Collette   He's gone, baby, gone! Fuck the system!

Brian   What?

Collette   The manager was so nice he said they're going to discipline the bouncer and make sure it never happens again, and he even gave us some beers to say sorry!

Sive   I'm actually really impressed by how they handled it.

Brian (*pulls **Collette** aside*)   Collette, are you serious? I fucking know the guys who run this place. They got us on the guest list, and now you're gonna throw a hissy fit over nothing?

Collette   Oh well I'm sorry, Brian, if me getting sexually harassed has ruined your buzz.

Brian   Oh my God, Collette, get over yourself. Would it kill you not to be a massive attention whore for just one day of your fucking life?

Collette   Would it kill you to actually stick up for me for once? Jesus Christ do you actually give a shit about me at all?

Brian   You are unfucking believable Collette, after *everything* I do for you, I swear to God, I put up with shit that nobody else would.

Collette   I didn't realise I was such a fucking burden. Girls, we're leaving.

Option B) don't report

Collette   Let's just enjoy our night, guys. Who's up for shots? Jamie?

Jamie   I'm ok for now, I'm actually not feeling the best.

Brian   Ah we're not at a fucking funeral, babes, cheer up.

*He puts his arm around **Jamie** and ruffles her hair. She recoils.*

Jamie (*in frustration*)   Get off me, Brian.

Brian   Christ, what is your fucking problem, I'm just having a laugh.

Jamie   I swear to God, Brian, there is a line.

She storms off.

Collette   Christ, Brian. You've upset her now.

Brian   Oh boo fucking hoo. It's called banter. It's not my fault if she can't take it.

Collette   Why are you always such a dick to my friends?

Brian   What the fuck are you on about, Collette?

Collette   Sometimes you're so disrespectful to them, like you just take things too far and I'm sick of defending you.

Brian   You're sick of defending me?! Listen to yourself. You are unfucking believable. After *everything* I do for you. I swear to God, I put up with shit that nobody else would.

Collette   I didn't realise I was such a fucking burden. Girls, we're leaving.

Scene Three

Rejoin here after chosen outcome.

Sive (*to audience*)   So we're back on the mean streets of Dublin.

Collette   I actually can't deal with Brian. I don't how it's possible to love someone and hate someone this fucking much!

Jamie   Relationships are complicated, babes.

Sive (*to audience*)   Collette thinks she is the only person in the history of ever to experience such conflicting emotions.

Flashback.

Jamie *and* **Jerry** *lie in bed.*

Jerry   Jamie . . . you're incredible.

Jamie   Haha, I know right?

Jerry   I mean it though.

Jamie   I'm sure you do, Jerry. They all do.

Jerry   If you didn't know me at all and you met me down the pub, how old would you say I was?

Jamie   It would depend on which pub . . . I mean if it's O'Reilley's I'm thinking you might be a young-looking seventy-three, or if it's Blue Bar then –

Jerry   Alright alright! Come on, if you met me in the street, how old would you think I was? I'm curious.

Jamie   I'd think you were forty-four.

Jerry   I am forty-four.

Jamie   OMG nailed it, that's so weird!

Jerry   Very funny. I guess I was hoping you'd say late thirties.

Jamie   Oh come on, what difference does it make. Either way, you're still way too old for me.

Jerry   Nonsense, you're as old as you feel.

Jamie   It's funny isn't it. You're a silver fox for me, but for Mum you're a bit of a toyboy.

Jerry *is shocked and pulls away.*

Jerry   Jamie!

Jamie   What?

Jerry   Why would you say something like that?

Jamie   Oh come on, Jerry, we're all thinking it. It's the fucking elephant in the room!

Jerry   Look, I feel terrible about the secrecy of all this, genuinely, the guilt it . . .

Jamie (*kissing his neck cheekily*)   Awwww poor Jerry. Is it killing you? In that case we should probably stop having sex then.

Jerry   You know I wouldn't be doing this if I didn't, if I wasn't . . . but whenever I think about it, I dunno . . . I, you're just so irresistible. It's like we're magnets, drawn to each other and I think we have a lot to offer each other.

Jamie   What like sexual favours?

Jerry   Jamie! Please.

Jamie   What? You have to laugh. This whole situation is totally ridiculous.

Jerry   Can't we just enjoy the moment. YOLO, as you would say.

Jamie *bursts out laughing.*

Jamie   Nice lingo, granddad.

Jerry   Watch it, missy!

They giggle.

Flashback.

Sive *and her ex-boyfriend* **Fergal** *lie in bed.*

Fergal   What are you thinking about?

Sive   Ah I dunno, Ferg. I'm just so happy I got into my course, I still can't believe it!

Fergal   I knew you would! You're a genius. Sive the psychologist. It's got a great ring to it. I just hope you're not going to start psychoanalysing me. That would be pretty awkward.

Sive   Well, it'll be seven years until I'm done so you've got plenty of time to get your poker face straight. It's going to be amazing Ferg. I'll have my own practice, you'll be a consultant, we'll buy a three-bedroom house in Dalkey and live like kings for ever.

Fergal   Haha, Dalkey?

Sive   Dalkey's mad posh no? Isn't that where Bono lives?

Fergal   That's the master plan is it, be neighbours with Bono?

Sive   Stop slagging me you!

Fergal   Don't worry, babes, I'll get us a place on Aylesbury Avenue – straight to the top of the Monopoly board, baby. I was thinking actually . . . when you start in September, I guess you'll be giving it up?

Sive   Giving what up?

Fergal   Well, like, you know . . . your work.

Sive   I'm gonna need the cash now more than ever. My scholarship barely covers my rent. I can't just stop working.

Fergal   I thought maybe you could go back to the pub again?

Sive   Fergal, to earn what I make in an hour now I'd need to put in a double shift at the bar. I just don't have that kind of time and I don't have the bank of Mom and Dad to fall back on.

Fergal   I know, but you read stories all the time about girls getting stabbed, or beaten up. It's not safe. I just worry about you, Sive

Sive   Baby, we've been through this. I'm always really careful, I only take on clients that have references or have been vetted through the app. All of my clients are really nice guys. It's not like I'm out on the street leaning into car windows. And anyway. You know I'm as hard as nails.

Fergal   Yeah . . . I guess.

Sive   It's just my job, it's work, it doesn't mean anything, and it's not for ever. You're the one that I'm in love with.

Fergal   I know. I know I just . . . it's almost like you enjoy it.

Sive   I do. More than slaving away serving scaldy ol' lads for minimum wage.

Fergal   You're saying you enjoy sleeping with other people.

Sive   Babe, relax. Let's not fight please. I love you.

She kisses him.

Flashback ends.

Jamie   Come on, Collette, we'll get you a couple of chicken nuggets and a can of Red Bull, the night is still young.

Sive   The night is but a foetus.

Collette   Eww. Seriously though, guys, I'm sorry for making you leave.

Jamie   The vibes were dead in that place anyway, babes, we're better off out here on the mean streets.

Collette   I just feel bad, girls. I have such a fucking talent for ruining everything.

Sive   What are you talking about, Colls, none of this is your fault.

Collette *suddenly perks up when she sees a tiny dog. She runs over to the owner – a scruffy, dodgy man.*

Collette   Doggie! Oh my God what a stunning little guy! Hi, little doggie, are you my little friend? How old is he?

Man   She's three months old, and it's a girl.

Jamie (*to audience*)   It's this tiny little baby pit bull. Collette is animal mad. She thinks she's the fucking dog whisperer. Half of me is thinking great this is just the distraction she needs. A bit of calming pet therapy and she will be back on the dance floor in no time. And the other half of me is praying this pup doesn't need a home. I catch Sive's eye and she gives me a look as if to say –

Sive (*to audience*)   I fucking hate dogs. One of my clients has this Jack Russell he brings with him every time we meet. He just kind of stares at us blankly while we're having sex. I'm like sorry, Rover, do you mind? I'm trying to work here.

Collette   Aw, little baby, hiya, what's your name?

Man   Her name is Sunny D. I called her that cause she's my little ray of sunshine aren't you Sunny?

Jamie (*to audience*)   Suddenly this guy comes out of nowhere and grabs Collette's bag and runs off.

Collette   Oh my God, my bag! He took my bag! That had my phone in it, and my wallet, and my meds! I need that bag!

Jamie   Oi! Sunny D my ass! You set this up! Get my friend her fucking bag back.

Sive (*to audience*)   Jamie's shoving this guy in the chest, getting properly aggressive and the dog is barking, and Collette is freaking out and I'm thinking Christ this is why I hate dogs.

Collette   I need that bag!

Jamie   Sive let's go after him. I can catch him. Back me up here.

Sive   You reckon?

Collette   Jamie, I know you're fast but chasing dodgy lads down alley ways is not safe, we need to go to the police right now!

Jamie   The police will never get your bag back! This is our chance.

Sive   She might have a point actually. There's three of us, we can take him.

Collette   Guys we need to call the guards!

Jamie   We'll catch him! I'm not scared of some teenager scumbag. Come on!

*The **Host** enters and asks the audience to make the following choice.*

Choice 3:

Option A) chase him

Option B) go to the guards

Option A) chase him

Sive (*to audience*)   I'm not sure if it's the dodgy coke we've taken, or Olympic sprinter Jamie's infectious determination to stretch her legs, but in a split second, somehow, the three of us end up pegging it after him. Jamie's powering ahead, screeching-

Jamie   I'm gonna get you you fucking . . . fuck!

Sive (*to audience*)   And me and Colls are doing our best to keep up with but Jamie's already streaking ahead. She's a beast. I convince myself I get good exercise, you know with clients. It can be pretty full-on at times. But after tailing this guy for two seconds I'm regretting not joining the gym.

Collette   I need that baaag!

Sive   Ughh I feel sick!

Jamie   I'm gonna fucking get you!

Sive (*to audience*)   It feels like we've been running for miles, for days, and even though I'm distracted by my lungs collapsing from lack of air, I can see through my blurry vision that Jamie's closing in on him up ahead. Jamie disappears from view and there's this horrible screech –

Collette *and* **Sive**   Jamie!

Sive (*to audience*)   And as we round the corner, we see this guy's pinning her down. He is literally on top of her, and before I can even breathe Collette runs up behind him and kicks him in the back. Smack in the kidneys. Suddenly he rounds on Collette, and there's this mad rage in his eyes and for a second it feels like time is paused. I'm, like, shit this is bad. Someone could really get hurt. But by the time I catch up with them, he's gone.

Jamie *lies curled in a ball.*

Jamie   I've got it. Colls, I've got it.

Sive   Jamie, Christ are you ok.

Jamie   I'm fine! I got the bag!

Collette   Yaaaaay!

The girls are laughing now and they pile on top of **Jamie** *and lie there laughing.*

Jamie   I'm a fucking legend don't worry about it.

Collette   Eh I'm the one who kicked him. Did you see that? I kicked him so hard in the back!

Jamie   Hello, I pinned him to the ground!

Sive   Ok, both of you are class. And I'm extremely unfit.

Jamie   Colls, check your bag, make sure he didn't take anything.

Collette   Tampons, meds, make-up, money, drugs, lip balm . . . phone! Yaay! I love you! I love you both! And I love you, precious phone. (*Starts kissing her phone.*) Mwah mwah mwah.

Sive   Seventeen missed calls . . . Brian needs to calm down.

Collette *stares at the screen, reading multiple abusive texts from* **Brian**. *She goes quiet and walks away from the girls.*

Jamie   You ok, Collinator?

Sive   What's up, babe? (*Pause. Nothing.*) Talk to us, Colls.

Silence.

Jamie (*to audience*)   But of course she doesn't. And it's bad when Collette goes quiet like this. Like that time in Valencia on our last ever 'gals' holiday'.

Flashback.

She's sleeping on **Sive**'s *lap, while* **Sive** *and* **Jamie** *have a whispered argument.*

Jamie   I can't believed she's ruined our holiday like this and now she just waltzes back in here like nothing happened.

Sive   Shhh. I told you we should have taken her to a doctor.

Jamie   Why, because she wasn't speaking?

Sive   Cos it was obvious that something was wrong.

Jamie   Doctor doctor, our friend's gone mute.

Sive   Jamie, listen to yourself. She was really upset and we just ignored her.

Jamie   For God's sake, she had a fight with her boyfriend over the phone, and decided to go AWOL. What is she, fifteen years old?

Sive   Brian was really nasty to her. He was accusing her of cheating, she got so upset.

Jamie   Well I wouldn't be happy either if my boyfriend went on holiday to Spain and left his phone turned off for two days.

Sive   This is different. I saw her phone, she had, like, twenty messages and forty missed calls from him, isn't that a bit weird?

Jamie   You know what's weird? Playing fucking hide and seek for attention.

Sive   She's depressed!

Jamie   I'm depressed! I've been looking forward to this holiday for a year! And I've spent half of it in the fucking Irish embassy!

Collette *wakes up.*

Collette   Can we go snorkelling tomorrow?

Sive   Of course, baby.

Jamie   I'm going to bed.

She walks off.

Flashback ends.

Option B) go to the guards

Jamie (*to audience*)   So we're off to see the keepers of the peace.

Sive (*to audience*)   The boys in blue.

Jamie   The good old Gardai Siochána.

Sive   Keeping our streets safe from unsavoury elements.

Jamie   Murderers and druggies.

Sive   Street walkers and escorts.

Jamie   It's 'trendy' to hate the guard, which I think is ridiculous, cos they literally protect us every single day and get no credit. Sive has a poster on her wall that says ACAB. I always thought it was a band or something but apparently it means –

Sive   All Cops Are Bastards. The attitude people have to the pigs in this country really fucks me off sometimes. Ah, they're a great bunch of lads, always looking after their community, helping to run the GAA Club and putting their lives on the line for the greater good. My arse. They're meant to keep people safe – but if you're a sex worker with a dodgy client, the only way you're going to go to the guards for help is if you're literally at death's door. People who say that keeping the trade illegal makes our lives safer make me literally Laugh Out Loud – it basically means if you find yourself with a 'dangerous client', which rarely happens thank Christ, you're tossing up a couple of black eyes with a criminal record. So most girls fall back on their yellow belt in karate or the chilled steak in the freezer. And don't even get me started on the trafficking argument. In what universe would you rather be trafficked into an illegal underground trade than a legal one?!

Sive (*To the girls.*)   I think I'll wait outside. I need some air.

Jamie   Oh come on, Sive, have you really got that much of a problem with authority?

Sive   I said I need some air.

Inside the Garda station.

Jamie   Excuse me? We'd like to report a bag stolen please.

Guard   Ok.

Collette   It's my bag and it's got my entire life in there, money, phone, medication.

Guard   Medication, right I see. Well I have a form here you can fill in –

Jamie   No like he literally nicked it off her two minutes ago.

Guard   Right well get the form filled in and we'll see what we can do for you. How did it happen?

Collette   I just put it down beside me –

Guard   So it was out of your sight?

Collette   Well yeah, just for a second, I put it down

Guard   You put it down did you?

Collette   Yes cos I saw this dog –

Jamie   The dog was a decoy. Like they knew –

Guard   And where was this now?

Jamie   On George's Street.

Guard   It's never a good idea to leave your bag out of your sight on a Friday in town, girls, you should know that.

Jamie   Great yeah, we'll bear that in mind the next time, but like this just happened, is there no one who can like pursue him right now?

Guard   Once you get the form filled in we'll look into it. And had ye drink taken tonight ye had?

Jamie   Excuse me I don't see what our alcohol intake has to do with this? We're reporting a theft here.

Guard   Now excuse me, my dear, are you the person whose property has been stolen?

Jamie   No eh but –

Guard   Right, so if you'll just let me do my job we'll get this sorted much quicker. So it was you was it, miss, whose bag was stolen?

Collette   Yes and I really need it!

Guard   I'm sure you do, miss. Now were you drinking? Would you say it was an alcohol-induced incident?

Collette   I had like two shots.

Guard   So would you say you were a bit on the tipsy side when you were stroking this dog then?

Collette   I really need my medication and my boyfriend will be trying to contact me and I really need that bag.

She starts crying.

Guard   Well now, miss, your little friend seems to be in a bit of a state here.

Jamie   Sorry, my little friend?

Guard   Why don't you sit her down over there?

Jamie   She doesn't want to sit down! She wants to report her bag being stolen.

Collette   Give me the fucking form!

Guard   Language please, miss. We don't tolerate abuse of any nature.

Jamie   She's not abusing you, she wants to report her FUCKING BAG STOLEN.

Guard   Ok I think you should take a little time out, ok girls? Or you'll be spending a night in a cell.

Collette *screeches in frustration.*

Rejoin here after chosen option.

Sive   We need to get a taxi ASAP.

Jamie   None of my apps are working . . . why can you never get a taxi in this town when you need one? Christ.

Sive   Hang on where are we? Jamie, aren't we just around the corner from your mam's boyfriend's house?

Jamie   Um . . . yeah he does live in the area but we're probably better off getting her home. The walk might do her good.

Sive   No we need to get her inside now. Come on, silver-fox Jerry won't mind. You've got a key haven't you?

Jamie   Umm, I don't think I have it with me.

Sive   Then let's be resourceful and ring the doorbell.

Jamie   It's one in the morning, Sive. He'll definitely be in bed. I really don't think he'll appreciate visitors.

Sive   Jamie! Where does he live?

Jamie (*to audience*)   This is such a bad idea. I've been avoiding Jerry for the last while because he started getting a little bit . . . much.

Flashback.

At breakfast, **Jerry**'s *flat.*

Jamie   Shit, I'm gonna be late for work

Jerry   Hey, have you seen the new *Transformers* movie?

Jamie   No, and I don't really fancy it either to be honest.

Jerry   Oh I just thought. I actually have tickets to a 9 o'clock showing tonight.

Jamie   Wait, weren't you meant to take my mam to that?

Jerry   Well eh ya, that was the plan initially but eh –

Jamie   Jerry . . . are you actually serious?

Jerry   What? I just thought if you hadn't seen it that was all.

Jamie   I can't believe you – (**Jamie** *is interrupted by a text from her mum.*)

Jerry   Ok, you're right. Cinema was a bad idea.

Jamie   Ok look at this. From my mam. 'Hi love hope work is going well. If you are staying in Jerry's this week could you pick up some bits for him. It seems he has the man flu! Can you get him some of the extra strong Lemsips and the apple pie he likes from Supervalue?'

Jerry   I am partial to those pies. But I can pick one up myself, I'm not that ill, it's just a tickle really.

Jamie   We need to stop this, Jerry, it's not fair.

Jerry   What?

Jamie   You were meant to hang out with my mam tonight and instead you're inviting me to the cinema?

Jerry   Oh don't overreact, Jamie, I just thought the film was more your thing than hers . . .

Jamie   We need to stop having sex. You can't pretend it's not wildly inappropriate. Let's just accept it for what it is; a midlife crisis from you and a tragic collision of Daddy issues and a dry spell from me.

Jerry Jesus, Jamie . . .

Jamie I have to go to work.

(*To audience.*) He rang me like eight times that evening. Probably from the back of the cinema. I couldn't face answering though, and I haven't talked to him since. Awkward.

Flashback ends.

Scene Four

The girls sit in the kitchen with **Jerry**. **Collette** *is hunched over her phone not speaking.*

Jerry Well this is an unexpected surprise on a Friday night.

Sive Thanks so much for taking us in, Jerry. I'm so sorry it's so late.

Jerry No problem at all, girls. I was still up watching *Planet Earth* would you believe it. It's great to see you all. I'm always saying to Jamie you're welcome here anytime. If you're ever in need of a good square meal. Not that I can cook! (**Jamie** *glares at him.*) I just hope your friend is ok.

Sive Ah she'll be grand in no time, just, em, got a bit intense on the dance floor.

Jerry You're sure she doesn't need to see a doctor? I can call someone if . . .

Jamie She's fine. She's just not in the mood for small talk.

Jerry So how are you, Sive? Jamie tells me you're working very hard, pulling all sorts of mad hours in the library. It must be tough.

Sive Well I really love what I'm studying so it's not so bad.

Jerry   Well from what I hear you're an A student, so good for you. (*Silence.*) And how are you managing financially, do you mind me asking? Are your parents supporting you, or –

Jamie   Jerry, Sive's parents are –

Sive   I'm not really in touch with my parents actually.

Jerry   Oh right I see, I'm sorry, I . . .

Sive   How are the wedding preparations going? You must be so excited?

Jerry   Oh gosh, yes very excited . . . and it's coming up so soon . . . and Jamie's been amazing helping her mum organise it and all the rest of it, she's really been a godsend.

Sive   Queen of organisation over here.

Jamie   Ah I haven't really been doing that much. Jerry's actually been very hands on, he's great, helping Mum pick the flowers. They even went dress shopping in town the other day.

Sive   Aw that's so romantic.

Jamie   So romantic.

Awkward pause. Doorbell rings. **Collette** *immediately looks up from her phone.*

Jamie   Who's that?

Collette   Brian.

Some time later **Sive** *is alone in the kitchen.*

Sive   So this house party has gone seriously downhill. Part of me wants to put in my earphones but part of me can't stop listening.

In the next room **Brian** *and* **Collette**'s *fight escalates.*

Brian I swear to God I am not in the mood for this. You think you can just run off on a night out and ignore me? I sent you a thousand messages.

Collette Yeah, calling me a selfish bitch.

Brian You know what, Collette, that's exactly what you are. How fucking dare you ignore me like that?

Collette Why because I want to have one night out with my friends? Is that so unreasonable?

Brian I'll tell you what's unreasonable. You making a fucking show of yourself in my mate's club, and then storming out like a spoilt brat. How do you think that makes me look?

Collette I said I was sorry, baby. I'm sorry ok?! I tried to get in touch . . . my bag was stolen . . . I contacted you as soon as I could, I'm sorry.

Brian (*shouting*) Sorry doesn't fucking cut it, Collette. Why do you have to ruin every night out? Why do I have to put up with this?

Collette Don't shout at me please, you always shout at me, why can't you just talk to me. Can't we just discuss this like rational adults?

Brian Rational adults?! Can you fucking hear yourself Collette. You're a bipolar mess.

Collette That is not fair.

Brian I am sick of picking up the pieces of your fucked-up life. I am sick of waiting on you hand and foot, putting up with your tantrums and getting nothing but abuse in return!

She starts crying.

Brian Oh and here come the fucking water works. That's right, play the victim card. Making me feel fucking guilty for your attention-seeking bullshit!

Collette   Bri, baby, please, let's not fight. I know it's my fault for ruining the night and I'm sorry, I'm so sorry. I don't want you to feel bad, I just want us to be friends again. I hate when you're angry.

Brian   You hate when I'm fucking angry? Then why do you do this, Collette, every single fucking time you drive me to it, and I'm sick of it.

Collette   Stop it, Brian, please don't do this.

Brian   You're fucked in the head you know that. (*He throws her down.*) You think you can manipulate me.

Collette   No, no no!

Brian   How fucking dare you.

He hits her.

Sive (*to audience*)   I really, really hate fights.

Flashback.

Sive *and her ex-boyfriend* **Fergal**.

Sive   Well what is it, Fergal? What are you trying to tell me?

Fergal   I . . .

Sive   Just spit it out!

Fergal   I . . . I slept with someone else.

Sive   What? Who?

Fergal   With Leanne.

Sive   Leanne?! . . . are you serious?

Fergal   I'm sorry

Sive   I knew it. *I knew* it, I always knew there was something between you. When?

Fergal   Look, Sive, do we really have to go into details?

Sive When?

Fergal Two weeks ago.

Sive Two weeks ago? Nice. Where?

Fergal Look it just happened right . . . it wasn't . . .

Sive Where did you fuck her? Your house or hers? A hotel room?

Fergal Come on, does it really matter?

Sive Yes it matters because you have just broken my heart.

Fergal I'm sorry, but you can't act like this is out of the blue, things have been off with us for a long time.

Sive What?

Fergal I know I shouldn't have slept with her, and I regret it, I really do, but I think we have bigger problems.

Sive Bigger problems than you shagging your colleague? What the fuck are you on about, Fergal?

Fergal Don't give me that, Sive! You fuck other people all the fucking time.

Sive No. no. Do not do this. It's my *job* Fergal, how many times do I have to tell you, it's how I make a living, it has nothing to do with our relationship.

Fergal It has everything to do with our relationship. Fair enough, you were on the breadline, it was an easy way to make cash for college. But it's been years, Sive. I've asked you to stop, I've offered you money and you just –

Sive I don't want your fucking money, Fergal! You have no idea what it's like to have no one, to have no one in the world looking out for you. I've had to rely on myself, I've had to work hard, I've never had support, never had a family.

Fergal Here we go again! It's always you out there in the cruel world, going it alone. Don't you get it! I wanted to be your family, Sive! I wanted to be that for you and you threw it back in my face!

Sive I can't believe this.

Fergal You push me away, it's like you only ever let me get so close and then there's this wall.

Sive Get out.

Fergal I'm sorry, Sive.

Sive I said get out!

Flashback ends.

Jamie *and* **Jerry** *are in another room.*

Jerry Jamie . . .

Jamie Look I'm sorry, work was completely mental, and then that night my exec Mike took a bunch of clients from Shanghai out to dinner and forgot his company card and was refusing to pay on his personal Amex –

Jerry Jamie I –

Jamie And I'm like don't worry Mike I have no personal life whatsoever, I'll just Uber to the office, then Uber to your fucking steakhouse, then Uber home and still be back at my desk at 7 a.m. sifting through your emails.

Jerry I think I should call off the wedding.

Jamie What?

Jerry I can't do this, Jamie. I can't stop thinking about you and I know that this, us, is so new but I can't stop thinking what if . . . what if we deserve a chance what if . . . what if I'm making a terrible mistake?

Jamie Jerry. Do you remember your life three years ago? Before you met my mam?

Jerry Well that's exactly it. You changed my life.

Jamie For fuck sake, Jerry, my *mam* changed your life. Before you met her you were living alone in that crummy flat above the Paddy Powers eating microwave meals and getting pissed every night of the week with your other divorced friends. My mam took you in, she cleaned you up, she's dragged you out of the fucking gutter. She reinvented you.

Jerry I know, I know and I am eternally grateful to her. She gave me so much. Without her, I never would have met you.

Jamie Please, Jerry, don't this is –

Jerry I'm serious! Compared to what I feel for you, I . . . your mam and I . . . We're not in love the way we are.

Jamie We are not in love, Jerry! You and my mam, you make each other laugh, you have a life together, you're building a house together in the south of France! *Christ*, can't men ever be happy with what they've actually got?

Jerry Oh so I'm just an ungrateful arsehole am I? And you're what? An innocent victim?

Jamie Excuse me?

Jerry How can you stand there and make out like I'm some selfish bastard? You're the one who started all of this!

Jamie Ok, I'm not having this conversation, Jerry.

Jerry Oh that's convenient yeah. Don't try and tell me you don't feel anything for me because I know that you do. Have you forgotten Christmas? I tried to break things off and you were the one who refused! You fought for us!

Jamie That's in the past, ok.

Jerry   You're unbelievable. You hounded me for weeks, called my office every fucking day, I tried to move on, and now that I'm here, where you want me, you're going to turn around and tell me it never meant anything? Is this some kind of game for you? You think you can mess me around and then expect me to just disappear?!

Sive *enters.*

Sive   Guys, sorry to interrupt but Collette's gone. We need to leave.

Scene Five

The girls' flat.

Sive (*to audience*)   Back in our house and Collette and Brian have taken their screaming match to the privacy of her boudoir.

Jamie   Sounds bad in there doesn't it. Like worse than usual . . .

Sive (*to audience*)   I mean I know it's normal for couples to fight but it's something about the way it goes from yelling to crying just like that. It freaks me out.

Flashback.

Collette, **Jamie** *and* **Sive** *are playing 'Never ever have I ever'.*

Jamie   OMG, guys, this game is so old school, I feel like we're teenagers again

Collette   That's the point. We are haggard no craic wenches these days, we need to go back to the wild days of our youth, when we actually knew how to get drunk!

Sive   Ugh no thanks. You could not pay me to go back to being a teenager again.

Jamie   I'm glad I didn't know you guys when I was a teenager, I would have fucking hated you.

Collette   That's so mean. We would have been BFFs!

Jamie   Guys, I was popular in school ok, it just wouldn't have worked.

Collette   Shut up you heartless bitch, let's play dis game! Ok ok I'll start. Never ever have I ever . . . had anal sex . . .

Sive   Oh *please*!

Collette   . . . that was actually enjoyable.

Sive *and* **Jamie** *burst out laughing and drink.*

Sive   You're doing it wrong if it hurts, babes, you need to relax.

Collette   Maybe one day you can teach me.

Sive   With pleasure! Right, Jamie, it's your turn.

Jamie   Here we go. Never ever have I ever been in a physical fight.

Collette *and* **Sive** *both drink.*

Jamie   Oh my God, you madzers! I used to have dreams about beating up this absolute bitch in my class in school, but I'm a fucking wimp.

Sive   I actually couldn't count the number of fights I've been in.

Jamie   We don't call her Sive the psycho for nothing.

Collette   I broke three ribs in a fight once.

Jamie   What? Really?

Sive   With who?

Collette   With Brian.

Sive *and* **Jamie** *exchange glances.*

Sive   With Brian?

Jamie   What you had a physical fight with him?

Collette   Oh yeah. It was pretty intense. I can't even remember what it was about?

Jamie   And he broke your ribs?

Collette   Well no, I mean it was completely an accident.

Sive   When did this happen, Colls?

Jamie   Ya what the hell?

Collette   Woah, chill out, it was ages ago. I just said, he didn't mean to. It was just like a passionate row

Sive (*calmer, trying to coax it out of* **Collette**)   What happened exactly?

Collette   I don't even know, we were just like shouting and stuff and then it got kinda physical and I fell against my bed frame.

Sive   He pushed you?

Collette   No. I fell. I don't remember.

Jamie   Why didn't you tell us?

Collette   Ok, guys, please stop freaking out, it wasn't a big deal. I would never even have known they were broken apart from I was at the doctor for something else, and I was saying it was really painful to breathe. Anyway. Ribs heal themselves it's all g.

Jamie   It's all g? Brian should not have done that!

Collette   He didn't *do* anything. We were having like a mutual row, it's grand. Can we just get back to the game?

Flashback ends.

Sive   Are you ok Jamie?

Jamie   Yeh, I'm fine I just . . .

Sive   Is there something going on with Jerry? I heard you arguing –

Jamie   No, there's nothing going on with Jerry.

Sive   Ok. It's just, you just seem really stressed out . . . and heard you arguing –

Jamie   It's nothing to do with Jerry ok? Something happened with Brian tonight.

Sive   What?

Jamie   He groped me.

Sive   What? What happened?

Jamie   I don't know, in the club, we were just bantering about me coming to work in his office with him and he properly groped me. I couldn't . . .

Sive   Oh my God. Oh my God that's disgusting.

Jamie   I know I . . .

Sive   Why didn't you say anything?

Jamie   I dunno . . . I just couldn't think straight.

Sive   Christ. We have to tell Collette. We have to.

Jamie   Woah! What? No. Sive, we can't. It would kill her.

Sive   Are you listening to this? (*The fight upstairs.*) This is an abusive relationship. I'm sorry but he's manipulative, he's controlling, he's fucking with her mind and she has a right to know!

Jamie   No, Sive, we can't please, she's so unstable it might send her over the edge.

Sive   She needs to hear it! She needs to open her eyes to what a dick he is.

Jamie   It's not our business to get involved. It's her life, she has to make her own choices. Just because she has all these issues doesn't mean we are entitled to interfere in everything she does.

Sive   This has nothing to do with her issues. This has to do with Brian sexually assaulting you and getting away with it!

Jamie   Can you just for once get down off your moral high horse! I want what's best for Collette and telling her will destroy her.

The **Host** *enters and asks the audience to make the following choice.*

Choice 4:

Option A) tell her

Option B) don't tell her

Option A) tell her

Collette *sits with her back to the audience as* **Jamie** *and* **Sive** *knock on her door.*

Sive   Colls? Are you ok? We just heard Brian leave.

Jamie   Collette?

Silence.

Sive   There's something that we need to tell you, can we come in?

They look at each other and go in. **Collette** *finally turns around; her face is bruised. When she speaks she talks in a flat deadpan tone.*

Sive   Oh my God . . .

Collette *stares blankly at them.*

Collette   What?

Jamie   Babe, your face is –

Sive *goes to touch her.*

Collette   Don't.

Sive   Oh my God, I'm sorry, did he do this to you?

Collette   What do you want to tell me?

Jamie   Listen Colls, let's just –

Collette (*shouting*)   What do you want to tell me?

Jamie   Tonight . . . in Rubex . . . When I was at the bar with Brian – he groped me.

Collette   What?

Jamie   I didn't know whether I should tell you but we just –

Collette   You're a fucking liar. Get out of my room.

Jamie   Why would I make that up?

Collette   I don't know. Cos you're jealous? Cos you've always fancied Brian?

Jamie   What?

Collette   I see how you look at him. Do you think I'm stupid? You're actually pathetic. Get the fuck out of my room.

Jamie   Do you think I wanted to tell you this?! I am trying to protect you from a guy who clearly is not good for you!

Collette   How would you know what's good for me?

Jamie   He hits you. He feels up your friends. Fucking open your eyes, Collette! You need to be with someone who treats you properly. What is your problem?

Collette   What's *my* problem? What's *your* problem, Jamie, you're the one who's fucking her mum's boyfriend.

Sive   What?

Jamie   Shut up, Collette, you don't know what you're talking about.

Collette (*getting in* **Jamie***'s face*)   Your little secret's out, Jamie. You're always banging on about how thin the walls are, well guess what? It works both ways. I hear you on the phone to him. You think you're so perfect and together with your swanky office job and your thirty euro manicures but, actually, you're so desperate you're shagging your mum's boyfriend! You're disgusting!

The girls fight – ending with **Collette** *fatally hitting her head. She lies on the floor, dead.*

Option B) don't tell her

Collette *overhears* **Sive** *and* **Jamie** *talking.*

Sive   You're probably right. Now is not the time.

Jamie   I don't think we should ever tell her to be honest.

Collette   Tell me what?

Her face is bruised after being hit by **Brian***.*

Sive   Collette . . . oh my God your face . . .

Collette   What should you *never* tell me?

Jamie   Did Brian do this to you? Where is he?

Collette   He just left. I'm not deaf. I heard you talking about me.

Jamie   Colls . . .

She goes to touch **Collette***.*

Collette   Don't fucking touch me.

She goes to her room. **Jamie** *and* **Sive** *follow her.*

Collette   Tell me what you were saying about me or get out of my room right now.

Sive   That's not important. Babe, did he hit you?

Collette   You're full of shit, you know that? I know you two are always bitching about me behind my back. How do you think it feels to overhear your best friends discussing you like you're a fucking 'problem child'. You're not my fucking babysitter.

Sive   Colls, you need to calm down. Just take a deep breath.

Collette   Do not patronise me, I swear to God do not!

Sive   Collette, you've had a really bad night, you need to –

Collette   Get out of my room!

Jamie   I am so tired of this.

Collette   Oh poor princess Jamie, it's so fucking hard for you isn't it?

Sive   Woah, why are you being like this? We're not the problem here. You're obviously really angry right now and that's ok, but I think the person that you're angry at tonight is Brian. What he did is really wrong.

Collette   Oh wow, psychoanalyst Sive strikes again, moralising me every second of the day. You think you're so sorted with your degree and your fucking left-wing politics but you're a fucking fraud you know that, Sive? You're a functioning alcoholic and you sleep with men for money.

Jamie   Woah, what?

Sive   Shut your fucking mouth, Collette.

Collette (*getting up in* **Sive***'s face*)   I've seen the escort app on your phone. You think I'm too stupid and 'mentally ill' to see what's going but I know what you're doing and it's disgusting.

Sive   Shut up, Collette.

Collette   You think you're so superior, always banging on about your alcoholic mam, but you're gonna end up the exact same. You drink every day. You're a hypocrite and a fucking whore.

The girls fight – ending with **Collette** *fatally hitting her head. She lies on the floor, dead.*

Scene Six

Jamie *and* **Sive** *address the audience.*

Sive   I don't think I'd ever experienced shock before that moment.

Jamie   I thought I was going to vomit.

Sive   I genuinely felt like I wasn't even there.

Jamie   Me and Sive just stood there for the longest time, and then Sive says . . .

Sive (*to* **Jamie**)   If you were the guards and you walked in here what would you think?

Jamie   What do you mean?

Sive   Brian's stuff is everywhere.

Jamie   So?

Sive   His bag, his drugs, that's his phone. He left his fucking phone here.

Jamie   What are you on about?

Sive   He was out drinking and doing drugs all night, they were fighting, he beat her up – it probably wasn't the first time . . .

Jamie   Sive, what are you trying to say?

Sive   I'm just saying, he's only been gone five minutes, and it looks . . . it looks –

Jamie   Sive, we need to call someone, we need to do something.

Sive We were out all night, they had a massive row, we came back here, we could hear them screaming at each other, Brian stormed out, we came in to check on her and . . . we found her like this.

Jamie Have you completely lost your mind? Are you actually suggesting . . . Brian had nothing to do with this.

Sive Think about it, Jamie. It's Brian who got her in this state. It's Brian who fed her drugs, Brian who fucked with her head, Brian who has been abusing her for years, Brian who slapped her around tonight.

Jamie You're mad. You've lost your mind.

Sive Everything that's happened tonight . . . Brian, the bouncer . . . the thug [the guards], everything, everyone that's brought us here, it's all been dickhead *men* Jamie, and why, why do we have to take the hit for it every single time? I can't take it anymore.

Jamie I can't believe you're saying this, Sive, we can't –

Sive We might have fucked up, Jamie, but we did everything we could to protect Collette!

Jamie *cries.*

Sive Do you know what's going to happen? [You/I] are going to go to jail. [Your/My] life is going to be over and for what? Brian will go to the funeral and he'll say how it's so sad, how Collette was just so broken that even his love couldn't fix her and it was always going to end in tragedy, and he'll go on abusing other girls for the rest of his life as though nothing ever happened. And there's a million other Brians out there who *did* do this, who are responsible for so much pain and hurt and cruelty, and they are never, ever punished. So why not Jamie? Why not this once?

The **Host** *enters and asks the audience to make the following choice.*

Choice 5:

Option A) admit what they did

Option B) say nothing

Option A) admit what they did

Jamie/Sive   I try and visit her once a month. She looks like death and we don't have much to talk about but it's the least I can do. I bring her in books and stuff. I don't mention the bruises, or how skinny she is. Brian's engaged now. It make me sick.

Jamie/Sive   I replay that night over and over again. Could we have done things differently? I couldn't have lived with myself if I hadn't pleaded guilty. It's only right that I do my time, and when I get out, I can pick up the pieces and move on.

Jamie/Sive   The worst thing is how pointless is is. She's sitting in a cell twenty hours a day and for what? Collette's never coming back. [Jamie/Sive] tortures herself over that night, I know she does. But the truth is, with every decision we made we were trying to protect Collette. We loved her.

Option B) say nothing

Sive   The trial was the hardest thing I've ever done.

Jamie   I was so scared. Every second we were sure that something would be said, some new piece of evidence.

Sive   We met up all the time, obsessively. Almost as though we were keeping tabs on each other, checking for cracks.

Jamie   I was worried that maybe that would draw attention. That the guards might think –

Sive   We were grieving friends. We needed each other.

Jamie It was an open and shut case. And even though I felt sick for every second of it –

Sive   – the more the trial progressed, the more I knew we had done the right thing.

Jamie Watching Brian go down for it was . . .

Sive The WhatsApp messages he sent her were used as evidence against him in court. The things he'd say to her . . .

Jamie She had pictures on her phone that she'd taken of herself – of her bruises, of her cuts . . .

Sive It was going on for two years.

Jamie I don't know how she stayed with him. I never realised how funny Collette was. How sparkly and fun and smart she was. I've got different friends now, a boyfriend, a new job too. Things are good. Overall. But I think about her constantly. I always think I see her in the street. I don't think that will ever change.

Sive I'm almost a qualified counsellor now. I work for Women's Aid. Every day I see women who are being abused, and every day I think of Collette and I know that we always tried to do the right thing. Jamie tortures herself over that night, I know she does. But the truth is, with every decision we made we were trying to protect Collette. We loved her.

Blackout.

The End.

Bloomsbury Methuen Drama Modern Plays
include work by

Bola Agbaje
Edward Albee
Davey Anderson
Jean Anouilh
John Arden
Peter Barnes
Sebastian Barry
Alistair Beaton
Brendan Behan
Edward Bond
William Boyd
Bertolt Brecht
Howard Brenton
Amelia Bullmore
Anthony Burgess
Leo Butler
Jim Cartwright
Lolita Chakrabarti
Caryl Churchill
Lucinda Coxon
Curious Directive
Nick Darke
Shelagh Delaney
Ishy Din
Claire Dowie
David Edgar
David Eldridge
Dario Fo
Michael Frayn
John Godber
Paul Godfrey
James Graham
David Greig
John Guare
Mark Haddon
Peter Handke
David Harrower
Jonathan Harvey
Iain Heggie

Robert Holman
Caroline Horton
Terry Johnson
Sarah Kane
Barrie Keeffe
Doug Lucie
Anders Lustgarten
David Mamet
Patrick Marber
Martin McDonagh
Arthur Miller
D. C. Moore
Tom Murphy
Phyllis Nagy
Anthony Neilson
Peter Nichols
Joe Orton
Joe Penhall
Luigi Pirandello
Stephen Poliakoff
Lucy Prebble
Peter Quilter
Mark Ravenhill
Philip Ridley
Willy Russell
Jean-Paul Sartre
Sam Shepard
Martin Sherman
Wole Soyinka
Simon Stephens
Peter Straughan
Kate Tempest
Theatre Workshop
Judy Upton
Timberlake Wertenbaker
Roy Williams
Snoo Wilson
Frances Ya-Chu Cowhig
Benjamin Zephaniah

For a complete listing of Bloomsbury
Methuen Drama titles, visit:

www.bloomsbury.com/drama

Follow us on Twitter and keep up to date
with our news and publications

@MethuenDrama